Of All Places
In This Place
Of All Places

Joe Milazzo

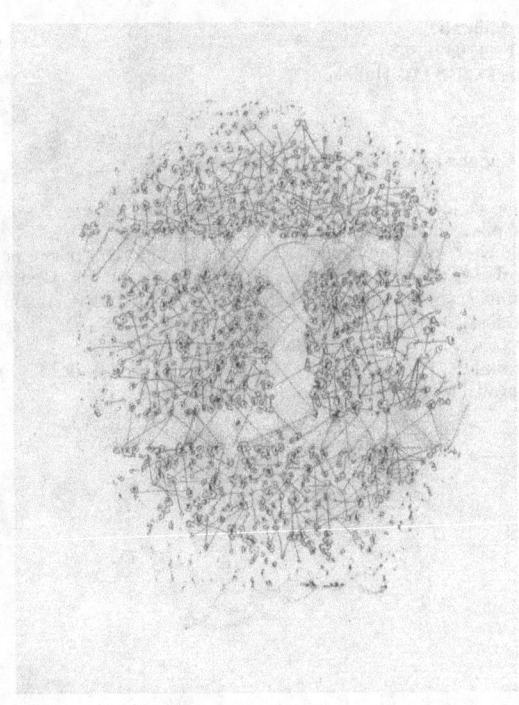

Spuyten Duyvil
New York City

©2018 Joe Milazzo
ISBN 978-1-947980-39-6
Illustrations ©2018 Lisa Huffaker

Library of Congress Cataloging-in-Publication Data

Names: Milazzo, Joe, author. Huffaker, Lisa, illustrator.
Title: Of all places in this place of all places / Joe Milazzo.
Description: New York City : Spuyten Duyvil, [2018] | "This poem incorporates
  language drawn from the Texas State Historical Association's Handbook of
  Texas (online), specifically, the Handbook's entries re: Dallas, Austin
  and the Dallas Garment Workers' Strike of 1934."
Identifiers: LCCN 2018002253 | ISBN 9781947980396
Classification: LCC PS3613.I47545 O34 2018 | DDC 811/.6--dc23
LC record available at https://lccn.loc.gov/2018002253

              sunrise is a trap   splintered
cyan   an aperture inverting
              black space
              sundown a manifesto curvature
              parthenogenetic
         belting cautionary LEDs   expressway's circuits

codes went into effect

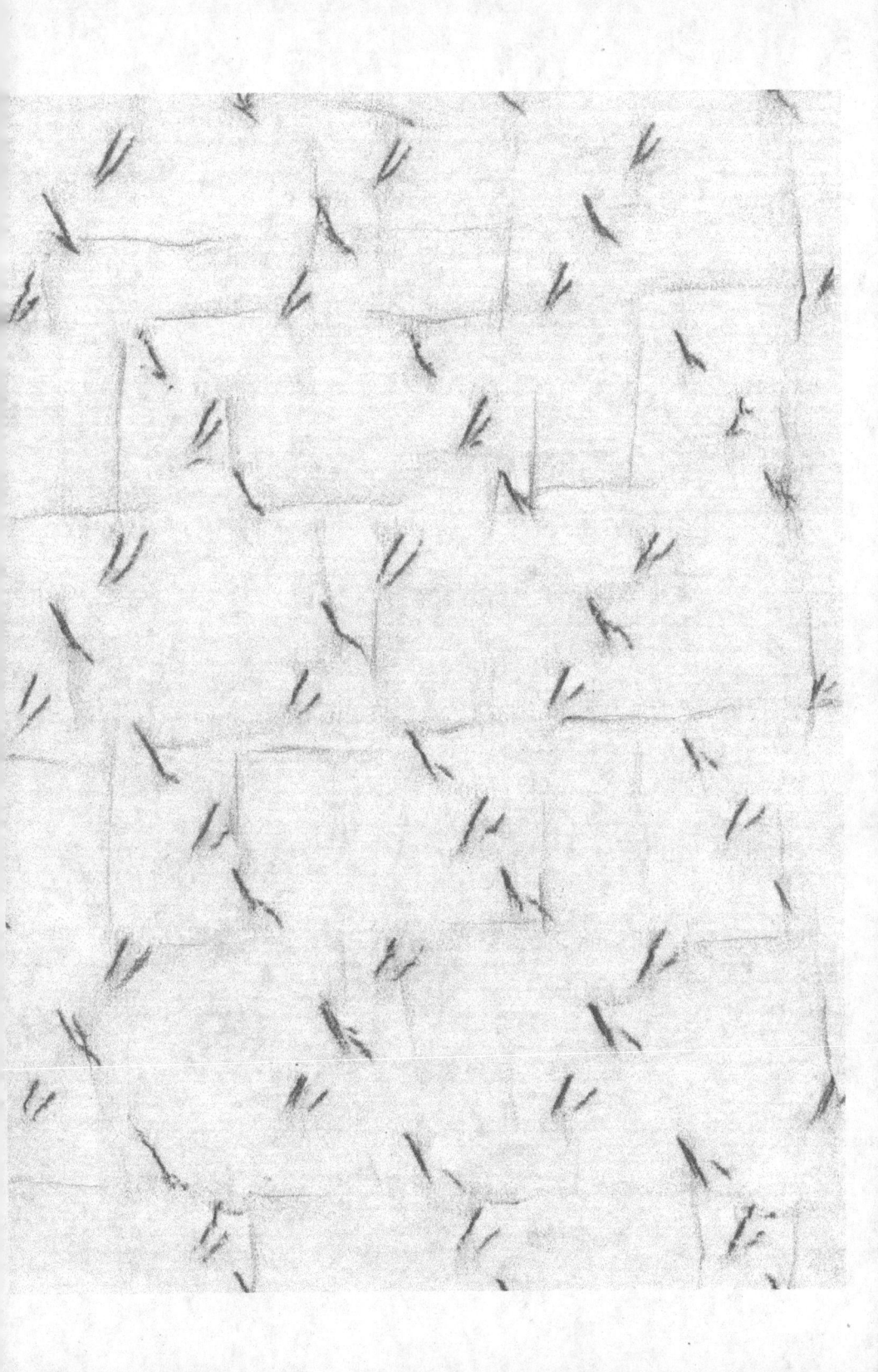

saxophone's nostalgia gold   cemented topography
                         of a sunken continent's high scores
     morning may i
          segregate   guiltless   what you matter
                                              to me

```
                                today i worked it out           today
        i grimaced pedestrian           counting out

                                        countdowns      ruts
of wind kicking culverts in
                the quarterpipe's eyes                          today
being like in being unlike      making myself
        a movement of air               a jingling scent toned          and all
                the usual               the neighbor's dog
                        a balloon popping       gruffness yelping
                out its little fright                           a day
        to pass         textured with the tasteful
crackle of a beige hypocrisy    creeping
                                conviction and a rush
        to understanding
```

                    am i responsible

for my accommodations

all that eventually comes

came within its corporate

arrests

      i mean the compromises
                                            that permit me
                                            occasionally a band t-shirt
                and to pose   myself
                      in the vintage sneaks   rolled
cuffs and slim fit
                        of this question   a question
      that isn't a question of what i'm feeling
      this isn't what i'm feeling   unshowered and sevened
                                            i'm not to be mistaken
                                                    not for feeling
                it's not my responsibility   to do anybody's feeling
                        for anybody   not for feeling's
    sake   feeling bounding infantile   slow   and

ended almost without notice
and completely without a strategic
geographic location or international
attention

             the how

                    of feeling   in chasing feeling with words   what
felt   neither called for nor uncalled for   the STOP
forces itself out into all four ways   as far as i walk
i can   walk
          affirm   across   the warrant of what emotion
dispatched to deliver me   a windowed envelope
with redactions instead of corners   arriving
with the weight of a parthenon   the noon
stops to coronate its scarcity   rays
lathering me with the assured
          madness of hours   psalming to our pampered saviors
of how over and over and over and over i go   and i go   go on
feeling   terrifying in the absence of palpable or

squalid terror   this isn't that
         no one walks beside   me   no one duplicates me   everyone
                                         fancies themselves an ombudsman
                                              a head
clearing in the air's banked pollen   smudged angels
their affirmation
                 blown back into the wind   flown away from
         the fish trappers   guardians   what of your visions
              of a decent minimum
willows in love with desertification   weeping irregular   why would
         they propagate here   when surely

the world center for
multistoried office buildings and
hotels protect the integrity
of the largest complex

we no longer live in a world of reign

             is there a man in that plane overhead   no longer
a child's question

but who   cut   that cliché out of my life
         and i am   aren't i   relieved
                 to miss the children   walking
their education's betwicts   boys in the form of limbs
dualshock joints   slithery
grinding   nails on nails   spastic bearings stripped
a bus stop   a doorstep turned-out   a mound of slammed backpacks
               guttered with an odd shoe
    i take my attention off the curb   into the street's hesitant streaming
          lauras and carolinas   féria black leather and kohl
                   thick as morrissey
               stretching hand-me-down death
to hem   unhappy weight
whatever

and is there something to be noticed differently
                in those asshole canvases
i repeat for the sake of anniversaries   in broadcast inflections
        sour lollipop snarl-up
        is there

                                                        but relief
            is to be relieved   not to feel its safety
i never
                        thought i was acting   unless to say as much
        as much will say   i never thought
not   of myself   not
of acting myself   never thought   thought is to uncover
some feeling
                    untransferably mine   a question
                            of misstressed position tall
        and presently   painfully adjacent
                healthy wicking   jogging
                            intersecting with post office complaints

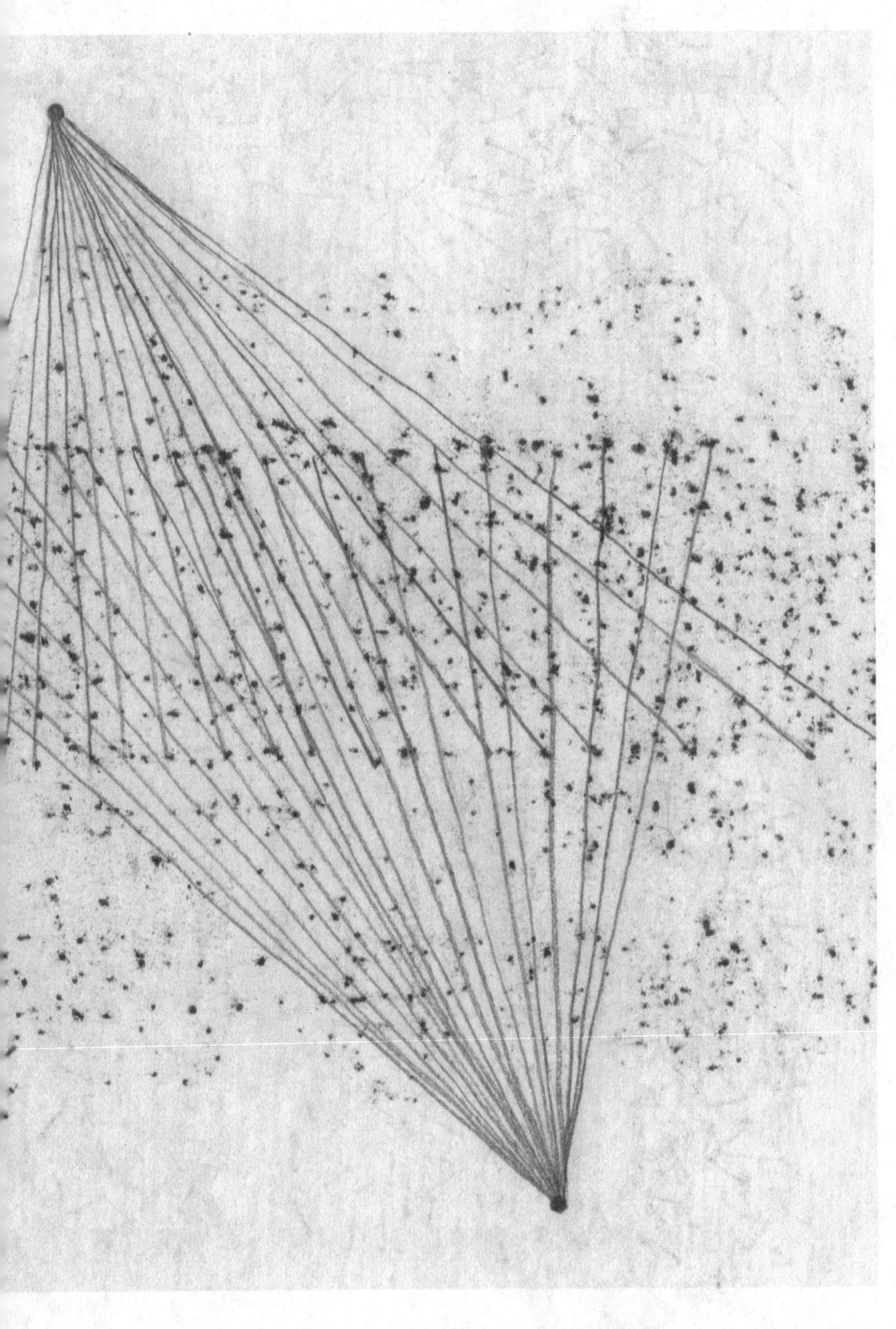

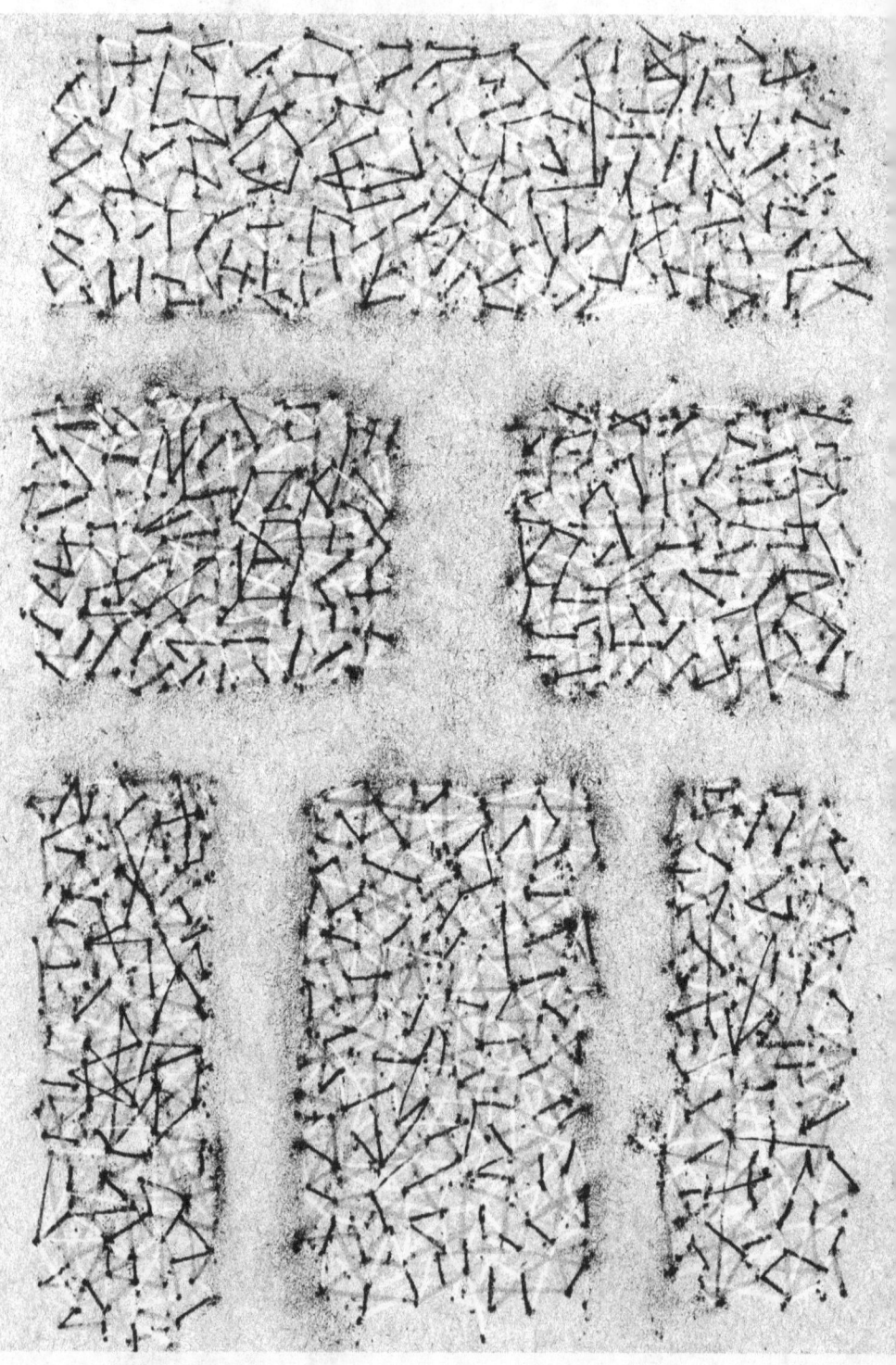

seeking to balance the
private guards for
on the east bank
she was hospitalized

    i powered myself through

        miraculous lunch   as if i wanted

            a massive engineering effort begun

                                        or somehow could comprehend
               to want to be feeling
some holiness in

            seeking to balance the economic development
                    long sought

                                            the form of an "again"

with the quality of ending almost

without notice and completely without

explanation

                        parousia
            having been set under the upholstery

                                            occasionally mine

as if i had planted planting

    in that neglect   munificent   and ulcerating

    there

with the ending

almost

without and completely

the quality of explanation

        tonight   the network is teaching you

to drink fatherly whiskey   to say drink

    in fact   when you mean enjoy

    wrapping thumbs as thick as the white

                                elastic band of porterhouse

      fat   politics thick and thin both   somehow

at the bottom of your glass

      before we clamber groggy through the

                women bit, kicked, and
                    beat law officers and private guards

      vacant spaces ruinous to our house
              we'll sit and pet the habits nibbling
warm in our laps   this is what we
        do not what we are
            we don't
        notice how existential our vocabularies
     are when they grunt the urgency
   of squandered time   which you say i'm
      almost always trying to   catch up to   i
read too rarely in your eyes but
                              i read today   read
for research   to be among the informed   not to know
      what happens next or
    after   what world did i   deny a nap
           what worldliness   did i gain   am i
     that type of person   sensitivities
         too carefully crafted

a more heterogenous character

completely without

attracting international attention

i harbor it   to be sadie hawkinsed   some antenna's ornament
                                  and there
be distinguished   too safely flapping adieu   adieu
my matching flames
           i bid you   behind the homespun glam   of who
                                              was voted to be most
     admired   eyebrows at the temples   gravitas chalky
and   random   aren't i fumbling
                at melancholy with the fretting
     of my left hand
              how i don't remember   not while   i observe

extensive promotional efforts

    how my memory congratulates

the strip mall   where our dry cleaning

  denies its chemistry with lavender

       catkins the slitlessness

coalesced at the end of a vectored buck's

     itching militance frictions

abundant

added

the small business

brickmakers, cabinetmakers, tailors,

milliners, brewers

completely seeking

and without a strategic geographical location

        around which the men with big

                checkerboards on their coats mill

      am i too circumspect   am i a remark

            alcoholic or uncivil   i secret in my ear a photocopy

  of a photocopy of an aerial

      photograph of the cyclades   hardly

ever do i order

      anything so fleshy with holding on   so humiliating

          as ungoverned desire   as paper

loud with creasing into which

            these things to do   these dawn swimmers

            sagging with age   lower themselves

                              and into analogous reflection

                　codes stipulating minimum wages

            unmaking our bed tonight
                 i felt

                     the wholesale long treasured
                       and maximum hours and

                     a blister smuggling its magenta
                     along the bottom ridge of my gums
a taste in it   as of a beer's head
                     or my commute's air conditioning
                         was it a day
i drank more water than i could afford
                     to criticize   and to learn
                                 you had something to say
            about your burdens   your vacations
                                 mountain- or ocean-bound
       like all dead ancestors' dead spirits

        i've been here   from the beginning   astutter

                  your shoulders slip   pour a cardamom

                      or some long hazel   a fig

   you know what nose   agrees with my instincts

but if you were   to name what you emanate

i couldn't hope to recognize that bloom

      as though another   name   some nursery heirloom

          pointed out to the littlest exhaustion in me   but never

                               no   not really observed

   unless a picture is observed

   to ease this inequality   towards moving what

                                    our   bodies made love

to the pavement with such force

with the quality of life ended

almost without another layer

of surveying patterns

   our tongues clubbing at each other

        mobbing tourette's of any field day

     or days afield   spirochetes   plasmids

water bottles   their intelligence in the underclothes   scattering

               to rags   slicking the floor

                   our stamina never blossoming or

     enduring whizzing transparence   just thrusting

                   until their leases were up

   maybe the seed   or a hair that leapt

            in from my beard

a cricket's leg

    insensate stridency

    wearing at the worn places   my mouth   mouth

prickled   a holly bush

       now sheds its kernel coat in you

           and your teeth are pressured to feel

their grain upon grain   the concussions

               of each vowel   every swear's grunt

     antlered lather

       either way   i'm not healed

                                       our bedroom used to be a daughter's

      just intermittently   or so we've estimated

by size and arrangement   counting

         up closets in the long time allowed

                 between our pleasures and alarms

beat out completely without

the idea at least law

officers stripped the clothing from

manufacturers attracted

a more heterogeneous character

a more heterogeneous character never came

talk to me you said

        don't cover your ears with   diagnoses   but
                 talk about what   my fantasy   self
psyche   what is there to lay
                 bare but decadence
an awfully barren
         radiant sameness anyway   so
            forked tender by the shale and semiconductor
reports whose sincere
                       intonations i don't want
       to grow familiar   spending
cuts   arctic   pulled apart   i turned
               to my side   chewed

the arrests

stripped the clothing from ten

migrating into the region

at least eighty-six women

without notice and completely without

reserves

      my words   to keep from spitting

             laughter   i laughed to keep

  from having to document   another placid instant

  involving all the black-eyed neighborhood boys

         sons of myiagros every one   who

in my not taking advantage

         of becoming then   become things

                     who am i with my renovations

in their midst

         my pta scowl   trying to disguise what my alleys

      gelid creek crossroads   black ice green

all the black santas   hugging parking lots

                           find feral for me

      deliver to me by way of

           the best spot for a trading post

           to serve

           printing and publishing

           to serve a striker's hands

impression   contemplation   negotiation

another momentary today outlasting   this aurora
            when i do not cease collecting   to wonder
        that mornings haven't turned into
                        telegrams   end-stopped and notorious
            architectures of mind   defaulted and biding themselves
                        into mere history
    a today
    of animal eruptions   here or there

sprinklers   bumpers   emblems in
      the old civic edges   snakes of spray paint   in the grass
            the more manicured   the inventories   the poise
      of television   what garbage of
            obscurely verdant magnolia wax   of tinglingly
                  peach magnolia woof   the north
                              catches out
                        the streets emptily arraying

bewilderment

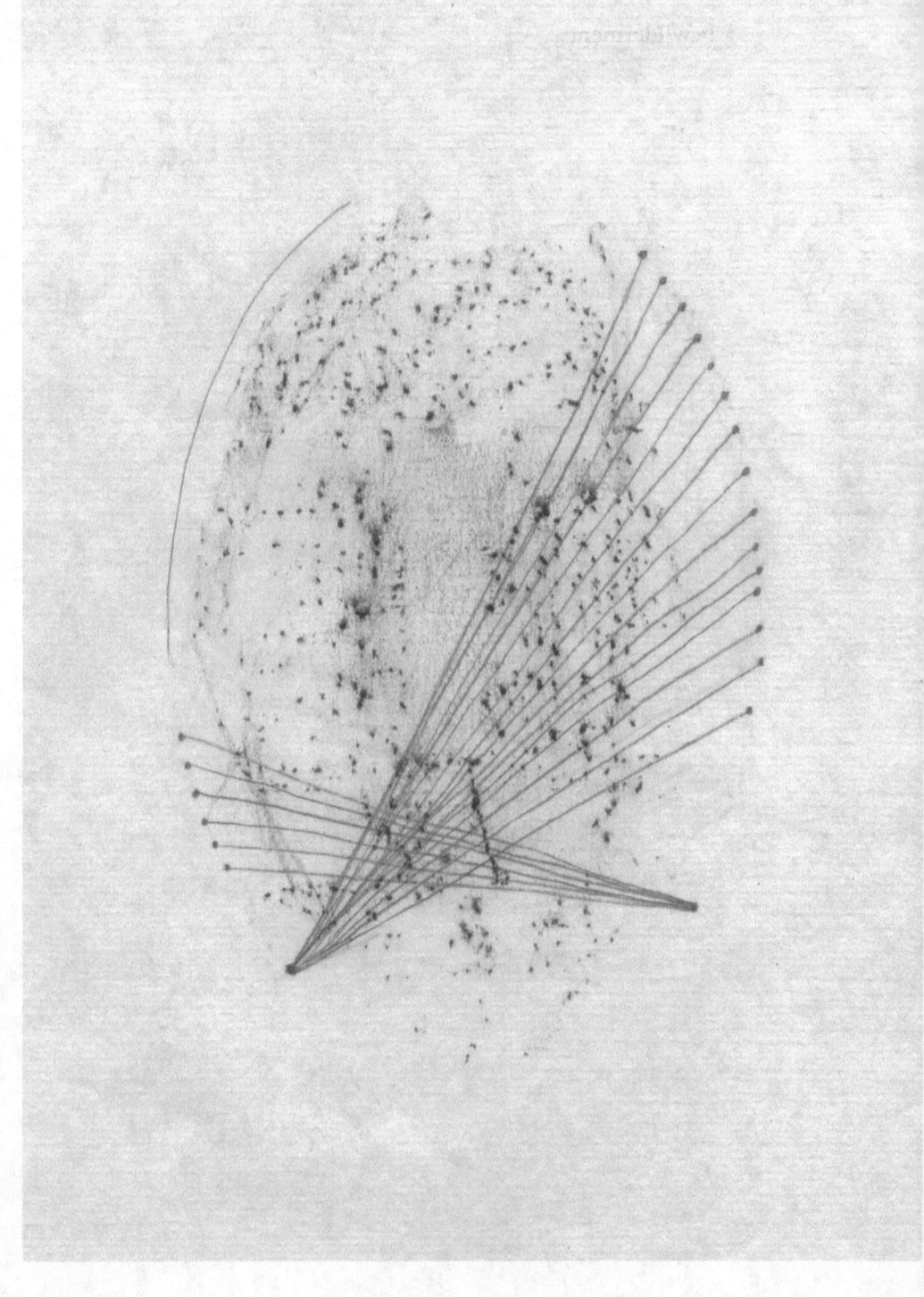

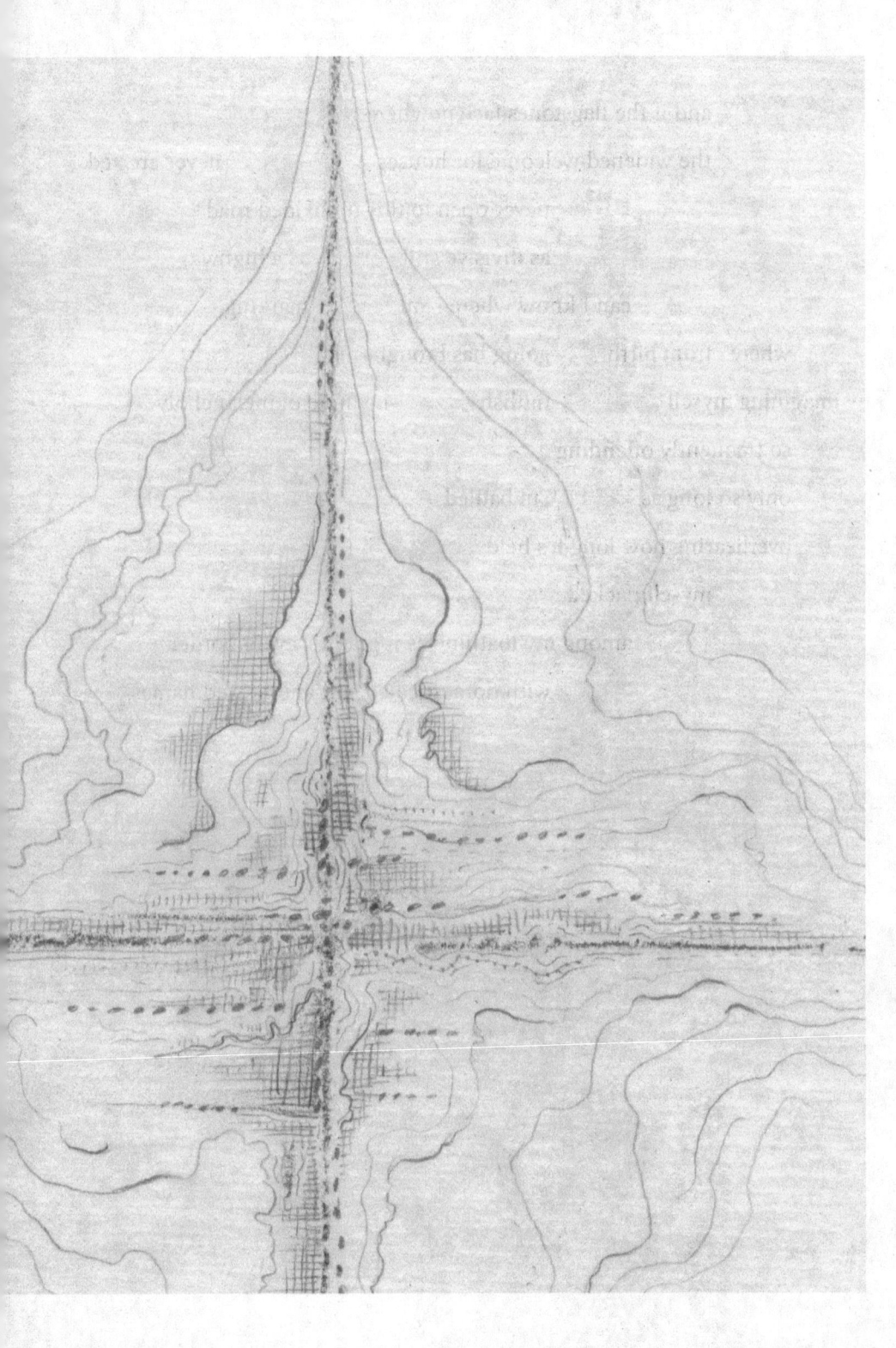

        and if the flagstones face nowhere

        the widened welcome for houses   never erected

              never open to this undivided road

                as divisive still   as a highway

          can i know where i am   marking

   where   from birth   going has brought me

by imagining myself   mulish   my note of melancholy

   so frequently offending

   only so long as   i'm baffled

overhearing how long it's held

      myself packed

            among my loathing as it graffitis every border

                with domesticated shit and brayed names

                women bit, kicked, collapsed
                    the integrity ended almost

if i could stake a briefing   on every lawn
                always so fluent   as my voice for myself
                    in ribbons of sandwich plastic

                at right angles to the river

i remember   that full spare nodding   away the avalanche's white
        idle   its actual lumbering
        a spayed cooperation   a daydream
of observance along
progress' rim   in the time it
    takes to flock into going
      into stepped accelerations out

            at right angles to the river
            attracting international attention

of care   a galaxy disclosed its throat
            the simple intersection of
    a handout and
                 the bereft week between
    the conference trophies
and that sunday   largely trademarked

                              the green arrows inch
                              forward towards cowering
                              or service   the auras
         of the covert as vehement   as uncarried cash share
he road and what the traffic

a massive engineering effort begun

completely seeking

a strategic geographical location

            of my accustomedness hallucinates   slowed by exchange's
prosthetics   my 10 o'clock   hand asphyxiated the waiting wheel
       my dream of volition suddenly so

                                                      ramshackle

                                                disrobed by his grime

            bowing his permission   his highwayman's

                                    assurances

i won't be plowed
       under curses exactly as i levied
            stalled out in aversion i pulled
       away from looking away from
                            the dusk rush's every microcosm

                      the small business
                brickmakers, cabinetmakers, tailors,

                    milliners, brewers

                    private guards

   their kings most kingly   striding in their surveys

always so consummate in their lapis

their brazen and flooding foundations

seeking to balance

a world center

           sententiousness pricks   and
remembering i did something today
                 maybe accumulative against this
cirrus grain   underemployed storms
the songs in the cilantro   and freed detergent
              the cigarette-red idled drivers
        smoldering   until pollution's show makes their knots
                                           come loose
       i chose a store   an entrance   i saved
    against my better interests   but   since i do it
all the time   this is no event
               it never happens   it happened only
    unsealed by bygones   halcyon or lovely or whatever
a broken cap that
      doesn't prevent its purchase   capital in that way

                                        the way of doors
                never needing a push   i yank   what i hope
    is that no unladen cart
            follows my plan far   into these rustic pallet gardens
    groves flattened by convenience   droning grapefruit
        no offspring   no forbearance   no primogenitors
in the zucchini
            a blood chill circling   my inflected ear
                only other souls
                skinning sinew against whine
                only stray candy   only
                voices sounding their cor anglais
ultraviolets languishing   light not vision   not heat

>   not utile   only this slanting
>   for everybody's awareness   springs at gleaning's
>   aromas
>   just what i've been looking for
>   for the path to any life
>   beyond this one
>   smells of the shaggy berries
>   whose painted faces grow
>   in the shadow of a tower
>   locked with a sword
>   swirling   crossed-up

in the world

follow the waterways

sprouted

multistoried

a hip injury

the best protect

                          the sacker who has nothing   cordial for his
          knack   can't keep the cold   with the cold
funny   he's   one side of our
                                              mouths when we postgame
                        our serviceability   at home in the terminal gasp
                        of a fictive gyre
                 i bought out the hours of the day
                 the reassuring madness
                        of the hourly
or   i cooked   or   i turned my reflexes on the phone
                 and talked it into the loneliness
i feel whenever someone   i cannot see passes through its throb

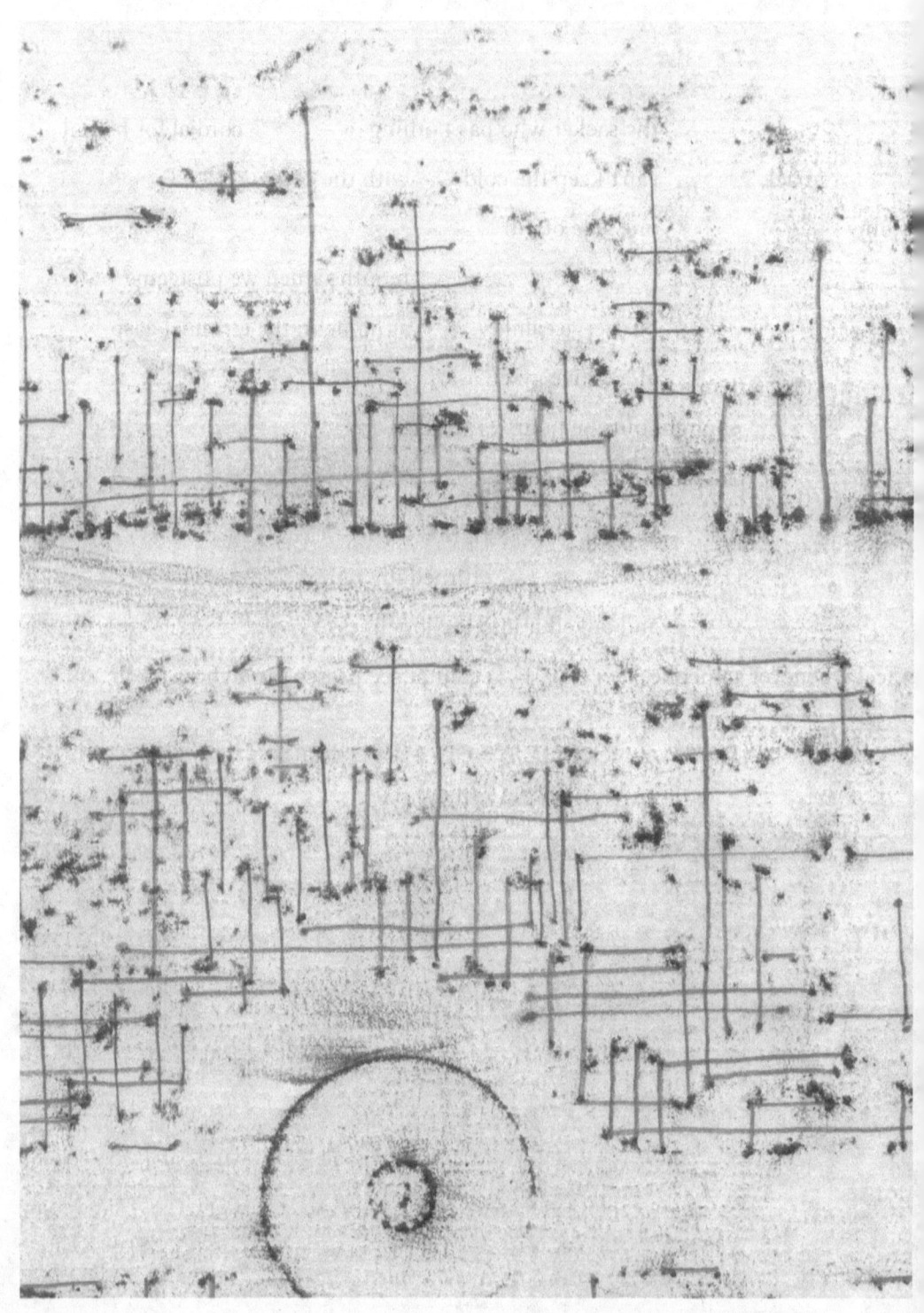

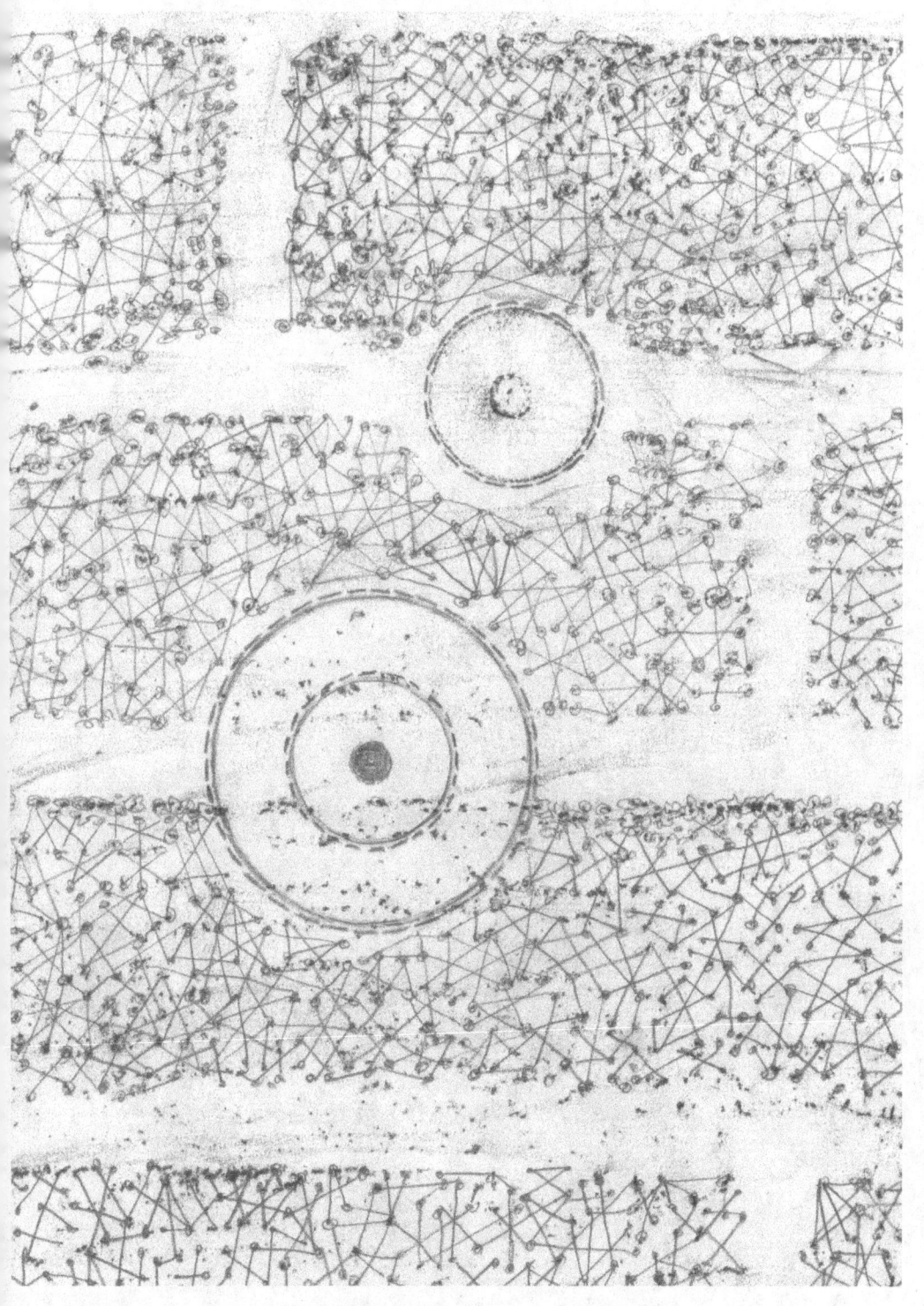

a union with such force

the three-story brick hotel

the buffalo-hide trade

a world center threw

you   volunteer   dislocating the ice from   its leaking
you clean
            my gravy chin with
                                    kisses   a filament
                                of burning   fiberglass
                    unease   timber for
this breathwork stoking   fogged
        mirrors with humid death   in all the privacy we have
                        we hardly need
                                        we pass it back and forth
            a wart burgeoning on the invisible
                        surface of our insides   a sore that
i'm convinced communicates our failure
                            to be more than what we achieve

       too tired now   bingeing on towels   will we fashion

                                                    a daughter or scold

            ourselves into a son   it's all

too desperate for its own job   good night   disillusionment is

               dry-goods stores, groceries, a drugstore,

            an insurance agency, a boot and shoe shop,

                 brickyards, and saddle shops

                     a weekly attention

     i can   i can fuck you   in the overlappings of never

                                  what can't be gone again

        drab blackouts walling in our walls

                with watching   we will be taken
back   the economy of
          proteins   autolytic scavengers   it's
          the tax of taxes
what thriving makes us
take for granted   when i was smaller
frightened
              of my own childhood   sleeping
          was still contiguous with prayer   an idea
              i had that virtue meant giving myself   away
hoping that i'd be rid of myself
              by controlling   such conflagrations of generosity

a temptation into sacrifice that saw

                    no end in breeding

         now   the happy duty of penetrating you   i see
how it all was a kind of
                  leading on   a self can't be poured so much
                                        only spilt   our lips plump
      with the pornography of the complaints
                                    we make over and over and over
and over   once more   more than once
the problem with politics is they're   obvious
even when   their subjects are all   occluded
stopping before coming   when we were multiple
             last   maybe in watercolors
not so much ourselves   screwed-up   or screwing up other selves
             never not what we can't afford   a molly-ed naivete
         decades stalled outside of consequence
                but the amorality of our more   queasy interlude
                      landslides   leaf and dust   restart

the first in the nation to
strip the clothing from ten female employees

the crawling

to conceive of the idea

the night shift fossils   the emergency haircuts
the gas card   both names

a natural ford
the best spot
the reserves in the ground
tore a striker's hands
and threw her to the pavement

straggle   wednesdays
                    and some thursday evenings   you'll have to babysit
          the churn of the garage   door lifting
a milky patch in the kitchen granite   the calculus of affluence
            is absurd and thus it can't
touch us   a pelt of dimes   doesn't dare rub me
                                    thus   therefore   i tell myself
            "i tell myself" as i signal   island-ward
                    under the piss of pump lights
                                            and a man neither dark
      nor light   made of hair and
            the colors of drugstore
      clothes   stuffing his t-shirt down
front before back   professionally   blank into
beltless depending   what strange sedentariness
      piloting is   stained
                  with vintage labors   the grease
      of meals blistered   foily   arizona gulps
      he wants to bring his map to me
                    or into the mutually assured destructions
of my path

and deflecting him is suddenly

        out of the question because of the sensation

    almost without explanation and

    completely without

    the quality of life long

    treasured

that floods the summit of

        my brain from the roots

           of my propensity to

talk   that deluge is brined

can i extinguish it   this hoarding

    in taking back every round

  iron ejaculation   every caesura

    every anecdote i've tried to improve

    by amputating its context   every

    invocation of pious obscurity

        every fairly traded allusion to my leisure

as some vocation

every paean to some city imagined further

        from the sanctities that detach me

from my dissatisfactions   my utopian

      lapses   every sentiment from which

    i pretend to eliminate conditions

sentiments which are only

      my own decisions

        leastways   everyone thinks

                      and everyone huffs at his or her own

contraband   everyone is a real

person   everyone else even more actual

        everyone

        or the rest of you   should i say

    the remainder from the formulae

        that heap us up in quantity

restart   return   restart   return   and rhyme
             remove this repeating curse

                         an insurance agency, a boot
                              and private guards
                                  abundant
                          the integrity of such force
                               completely ended

not that he can't read the map   only   it's not the kind
of thing he   reads
these representations   an idea for the improvement
                of everything   this being not his epic
                                    not his talk that vaults the city walls
inherently free
        never less than a gamble upgraded
                                    to a knock-off   demagoguery
    a fever of citizen celebrities   elliptical in their smart
                                                                houses

        square houses   "man"   doors like a painting
                      disappeared into another painting
                  every surface a smoothness
    white but pitted just a little   after a glide of leather
                    and wives unquote
their neutral headstone   faces   man
who wouldn't care to be addressed by any   explanation
    milk and diapers hanging on a job he'll be late for
    man   plaster   laths
        he points   fingertip   black as a grape
     a van with wire windows   laden maybe
man   picture the   music of his tools
as his workshop takes those road humps
doping deliveries with admiration
         don't dawdle   hang your solicitations
               get a good look   man
       not one street
west of the fairways   being a high street

of more heterogeneous character
of codes in effect
of regional products
she was hospitalized with
a law officer

             with his flip-phone   and   attested
       ignorance of how the sides
       here connect   he is auctioning
          off what it will take   man
                 to make him go away but
what direction will a limp dollar take him   what i could hang out
a crack of my window   charity declaring itself
with disdain   2 dollars
5
but when given in bad faith   blackmail
      denominations   why
                    doesn't intention invalidate this
     exchange   man   why does the transfer succeed only
       so long as we prop up the cynical
           view that the pale pinks and grays
                  and oranges submitting to

he grubby fruit of a questing finger

                       all scratching at the same fill-in compose

                                         not a common imagination but

    outline an imagined necessity   a necessary

               complication

          streets laid out at right angles to the river

          laid out at 45 degrees off cardinal directions

     no easy collisions   no flat collisions

          annexation of adjacent communities added

            another layer of surveying patterns

         city-owned greenbelts follow the waterways

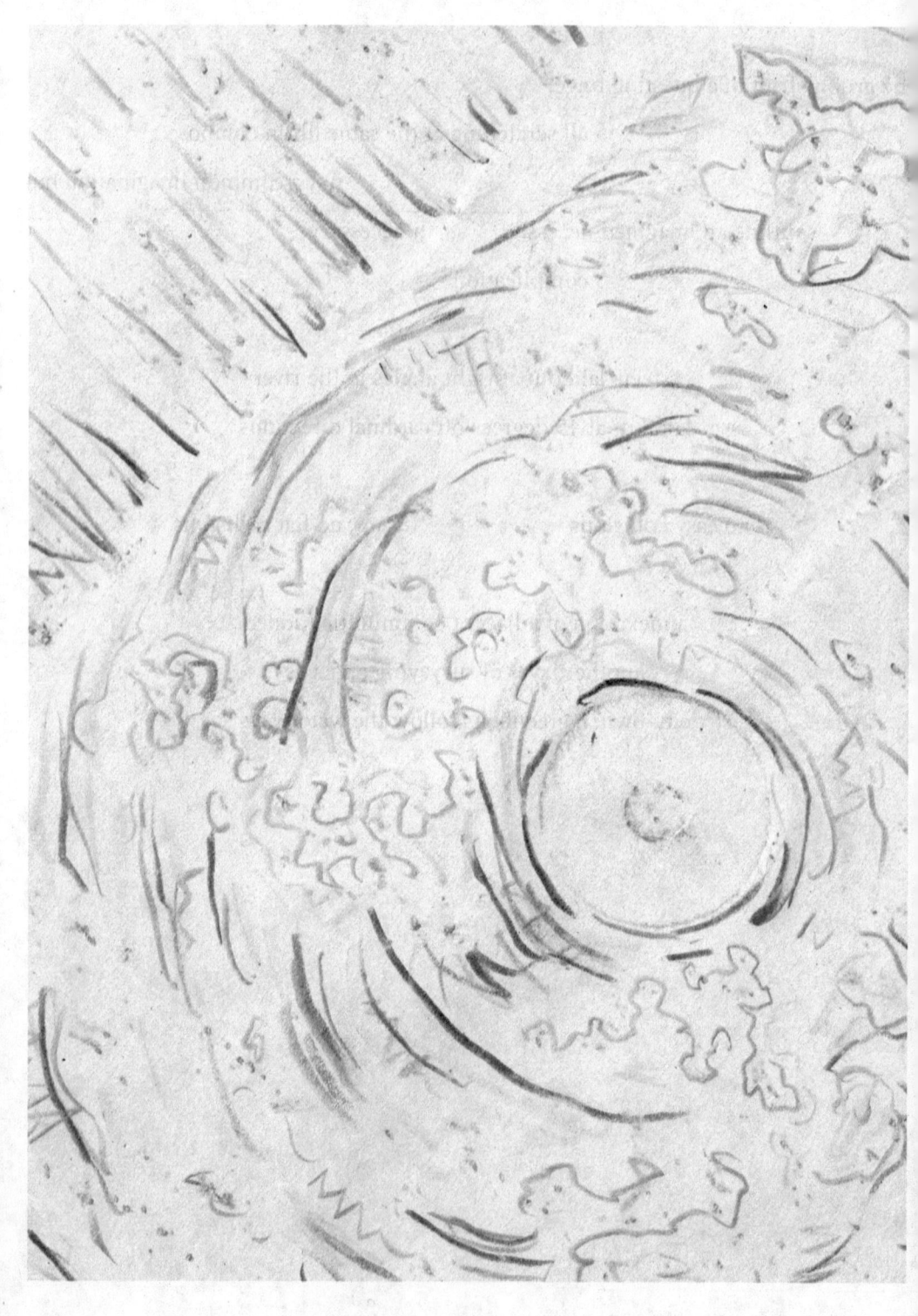

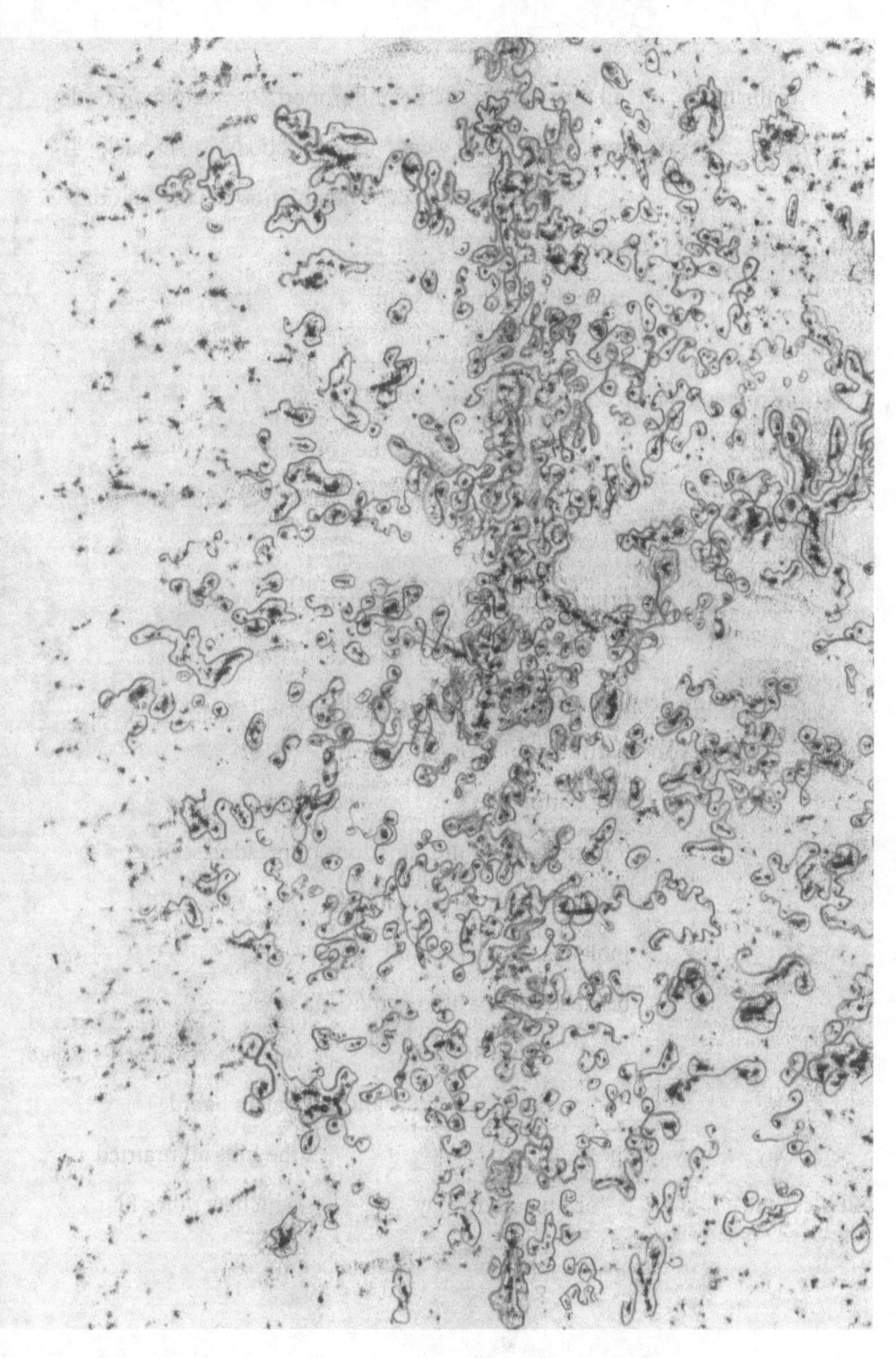

collisions   all over   the neighborhood   neighborhoods
 demarcated as what they were   neighborhoods   set back
    into landmarks   neighborhoods driven out
a complex of destinations you
  can either go out of your
way to avoid
 or pretend isn't recognizable from
   where you confine yourself
    to living   out past

  the integrity of their residential areas

 the deep woods of shitty apartments
 beyond partitions of drought unseen
 in all   that cotton   weeds
  tottering   illuminations of preadolescence
 play   tall through those clouds
  moieties   because
  because   little is blowing
   way out past   where acres of self-storage
    and rv dealers hoard
way   way out past   the hills all prairied
god bless me   man   or hurrah my day   whichever dies first

       maybe   my irrelevance matters most to me

                when it should matter less

                                      at best the least

maybe it's past time i called you

                and confessed to the mediocrities of

                                our thinking   we have no

lifestyle of which this is only one   unsingular

      pastime   all we annulled in

offenses taken for trauma

                what obsolescent   instrumental nihilisms

    nostalgia for hands wrung over conformity

too late to be belated

or not   i asked your forgiveness
           said   cabbed again   something has happened to me
                   something has made me live and
                              am i too backward to have taken
           you and succumbed and
                              violated you   as violently
     as only the childless are permitted
                        my palate ribbed with irritation   my cheeks
     sharper than the piercings
           of this mystery's infestation   can't you

feel it now   inflamed
                with improved expressions   molars bleeding
                                or weeping blood between
the floss and recession   mouth
                                a mansion gate lynched
on its own hinges   a charring
            creak   a fetus of fire
opuscule of hurt
            you had me at "plight"

                                        man   he never
         affirmed that he was lost   only
said he was trying   man   and
              regular unleaded on my shoes
i ask you   everyone   in your
conspicuous vestigial terror
         your long sleeves   stripes
         your skinned rutting
                        your private raging usage

        who, in other parts of the country, made as little
             as codes blocking the doors
         women blocking the streets the greenbelts
              an arbitrated settlement
           threw the ending to the pavement
       her songsheet explanation completely without

            your statuses as heavy
     with wristwatch brilliance as what i once
               thought spun generations away
  from each other   your ownership and calories
  your monitor   your lyrical opinions   their half-tones
presiding not in place of
              but in simulation of the sky
        at its most tenuous   differently abled
            yellowed with distraction   or pre-language
  archaic   pitched to "ye"s   thorns   unreproducible

    so   mornings   may i glut myself
         while your witness is so near   your flicking tongues

                     a world center for

              annexation of more adjacent

                heterogeneous character

                    a union threw

                    the dam collapsed

    so approximate

with your wheeling

        escape into this supplication with me   homing in

let us mow and salt   these tracts

                for no one was there

who will be there

        in the manner of an answered call

            a satellite promise

                                        guide us

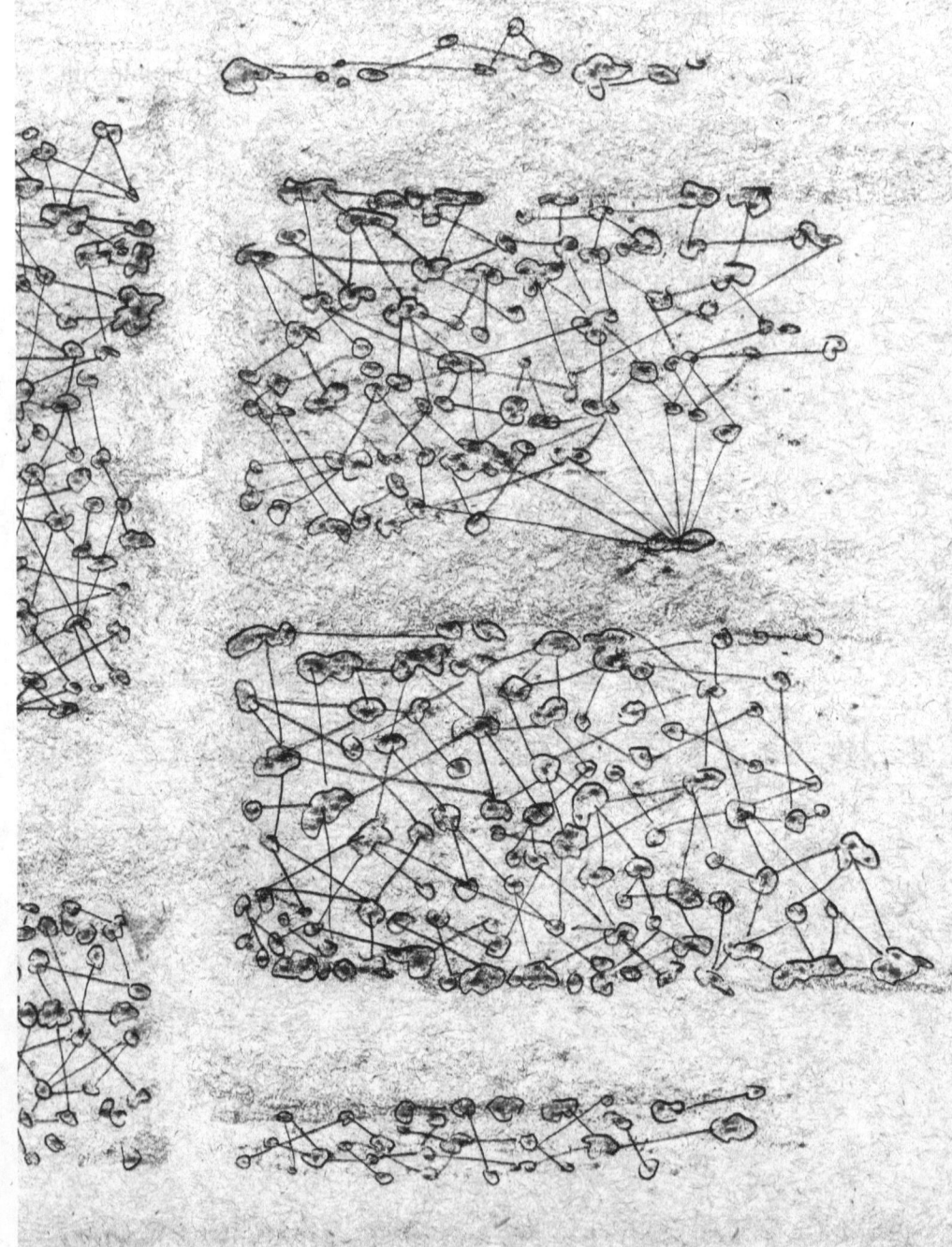

horned ball   hovering   ferocious
          light   strand all our abdications
                         among the pillories
                         scalped orifices
                         arms aching under the infant sparrows'
                         amplifying beaks
                         posts and boards   numbed
                                          unbending cells
          applianced   incendiary
their stiff forgotten parade   parading noiselessly down

our town

This poem incorporates language drawn from the Texas State Historical Association's *Handbook of Texas* (online), specifically, the *Handbook*'s entries re: Dallas, Austin and the Dallas Garment Workers' Strike of 1934.

The cover art and illustrations began as graphite rubbings taken from the Lorch Building in Dallas, TX, the site of violent protests during the Dallas Garment Workers' Strike of 1934.

JOE MILAZZO is the author of the novel *Crepuscule W/ Nellie* and *The Habiliments*, a volume of poetry. He co-edits the online interdisciplinary arts journal *[out of nothing]*, is a Contributing Editor at *Entropy*, and is also the proprietor of Imipolex Press. Joe lives and works in Dallas, TX, where he was born and raised. His virtual location is www.joe-milazzo.com.

LISA HUFFAKER's creative practice embraces poetry, visual art, and bookmaking. She is the founder of Dallas-Fort Worth's White Rock Zine Machine, a project that makes tiny books by local writers and artists available via whimsically repurposed vending machines. Her poetry has appeared in numerous journals, including *Southwest Review*, *Measure*, and *Poet Lore*. From July through September 2017, Lisa served as the C3 Visiting Artist at the Dallas Museum of Art. She currently sings with the Dallas Opera and teaches creative writing with community partners ranging from public libraries to youth shelters.